Iara M. Florêncio
Diogo C. Cavalcanti
Luciana L. Freire

Tourist app project for a deaf community

Iara M. Florêncio
Diogo C. Cavalcanti
Luciana L. Freire

Tourist app project for a deaf community

Prototype that meets the linguistic needs of the deaf community in the city of Caruaru-PE

Imprint
Any brand names and product names mentioned in this book are subject to trademark, brand or patent protection and are trademarks or registered trademarks of their respective holders. The use of brand names, product names, common names, trade names, product descriptions etc. even without a particular marking in this work is in no way to be construed to mean that such names may be regarded as unrestricted in respect of trademark and brand protection legislation and could thus be used by anyone.

Cover image: www.ingimage.com

This book is a translation from the original published under ISBN 978-613-9-67366-7.

Publisher:
Sciencia Scripts
is a trademark of
Dodo Books Indian Ocean Ltd. and OmniScriptum S.R.L publishing group

120 High Road, East Finchley, London, N2 9ED, United Kingdom
Str. Armeneasca 28/1, office 1, Chisinau MD-2012, Republic of Moldova, Europe
Printed at: see last page
ISBN: 978-620-8-15965-8

Summary

Thanks

I would first like to thank God for giving me the health and strength to overcome difficulties.

To my father Izaildo, the hero who gave me support and encouragement in difficult times, when I was discouraged and tired. I would like to thank my mother Rita, who, despite all the difficulties, strengthened me and who was very important to me and without whom this monograph would not have been the same.

To my advisor Luciana, for all her help, corrections and encouragement.

To my friend Ivson Luna (*in memoriam*), for all the questions he answered, for all the group work he did with all his effort and dedication, for all his help at the beginning of the course. And to my friend Aldenize Bezerra for all her patience and understanding during this difficult period when I was so absent.

To the interpreter Patricia, for all her help with the translations.

To everyone who directly or indirectly played a part in my education, thank you very much.

Summary

Due to the advance in the use of mobile and tablet applications and their importance in facilitating interaction and various daily activities, it is possible to affirm the need for accessibility to information, especially among the population studied. This project will study deaf people, accessible tourism and information systems, which will serve as support for the design of a prototype of an interactive tourist application that aims to meet the needs of the deaf community.

The integration of the social group of deaf people is of the utmost importance. They are fully capable of carrying out any activity, as long as they are given the tools they need. The main problem with accessibility for deaf people in Brazil is not only found in digital interfaces, the problems go beyond these, transcending the virtual and entering the real world: the lack of translators in sign language for orientation in public or private spaces limits the understanding of deaf people, most of whom do not understand written or spoken Portuguese in whole or in part.

This community increasingly wants to travel and discover new places, and tourism in Brazil is growing, but accessibility has not kept pace with this growth. It is necessary to enforce the existing accessibility laws, which are aimed at the inclusion of all individuals, and above all to ensure that the right to come and go and the right to leisure of the human being are fulfilled. The application to be designed will be interactive, containing explanatory videos of the cultural sights in LIBRAS.

Introduction

This monograph aims to create a prototype of a tourist app, with the objective of providing guidance on the location of cultural tourist sites in Caruaru, with a target audience: the deaf community. Since this population group, according to the data researched and subsequently presented, is a potential audience for tourism.

Based on this analysis, we intend to understand the needs of the deaf community with regard to existing information systems and test the linguistic possibilities to be implemented in the product. We will be able to use written sign language, LIBRAS signaled in the form of a video and Portuguese subtitles to understand deaf people at their various linguistic levels. The study of information systems is extremely important in order to understand how information should be organized in such a way as to ensure usability, making understanding quicker and more effective.

In addition to understanding the needs of deaf people in digital projects and the cultural context in which they live, the aim is to generate possibilities for better operation and understanding of the application, to understand the location and distribution of tourist attractions in the city of Caruaru and, if they exist, to insert signs representing the city's tourist attractions.

This paper is divided into three sections: The Deaf Universe, Accessible Tourism and Information Systems. In these sections we will understand the thoughts of authors who address these issues, for example: Skliar (1997), Quadros (2003), Laborrit (1994), Strobel (2008) among other references in the area of education and the deaf community, Almeida (2006) and Albuquerque (2012) in Accessible Tourism and finally, in information systems Padovani (2004), Lupton (2014), Barbosa and Silva (2010) among others.

Research problem

The lack of knowledge about how interface design can design digital applications that guide deaf people to cultural tourist attractions in the city of Caruaru (PE).

Justification

Deaf people are a linguistic minority, and in Brazil they use the Brazilian Sign Language (Libras). In Brazil, 9.7 million people have some form of hearing loss (IBGE, 2010). For deaf people, the process of learning to read and write Portuguese is complicated, and many are considered to be functionally illiterate, as they do not understand Portuguese in its written form.

This difficulty in learning Portuguese is due to the fact that deaf people understand the world through sight and Portuguese is based on phonetic sounds. The language that suits the visual needs of deaf Brazilians is LIBRAS (Brazilian Sign Language), and it is essential to use it to learn Portuguese as a second language.

There are many reasons why learning Portuguese is so difficult, whether it's the lack of knowledge of LIBRAS as a first language, the shortcomings of the Brazilian education system, which doesn't have a sufficient number of interpreters from oral language to sign language, or the alarming numbers of deaf school dropouts who don't adapt to the exclusively oral education system. Methods that make it easier for deaf people to be independent in their day-to-day tasks are sure to generate huge gains in the quality of life of this community, such as tourism.

Tourism is a fundamental economic activity for Brazil, and especially for the Northeast. Caruaru's tourism stands out for its cultural potential linked to Pernambuco's popular culture. The city has the largest free market in Brazil and "the largest center of figurative arts in the Americas", according to UNESCO (United Nations Educational, Scientific and Cultural Organization) apud Lira (2008). It is also only 51 km from the village of Fazenda Nova in the municipality of Brejo da Madre de Deus, where the largest open-air theater in the world is located. Every year at Easter time, the well-known Passion of Christ is performed at the theater in New Jerusalem, which attracts people from all over the world to watch the performance.

Caruaru's Sao Joao festivities are also a potential tourist attraction, as the city is known and often referred to as the "capital of forró". In 2015, according to data from the city government, it welcomed 1.8 million tourists over the 30 days of the festivities. Caruaru City Hall already provides a LIBRAS interpreter to translate some of the bands performing at Sao Joao de Caruaru, facilitating the inclusion of deaf people in this great local festival. (PREFEITURA DE CARUARU, 2015)

Apps for smartphones and tablets have been gaining ground and popularity. These apps can have the most diverse uses, depending on the purpose for which they are proposed. Since this application is designed to be informational, it is of great value, as it is updatable and portable, all you need is a cell phone or tablet with the necessary settings. Information is a basic point in the development of tourism, AZEVEDO (1999) explains that the topic must have scientific and social relevance. As we have seen so far, we can say that research has the necessary scientific and social importance, as well as marketing importance, because there is a target audience that needs the final product. Finally, in order for information to be clearly understood by deaf people, research is needed into measures that can be used to facilitate this understanding.

General objective

Propose a prototype of an interactive application for the location of tourist attractions in Caruaru, for tourists in general or deaf Caruaruenses.

Specific objectives

Understanding the graphic needs of deaf people to understand the context of an interactive cultural tourism application.

Generate alternatives for the best possible understanding of the graphic piece to be created.

Point out the most visited tourist attractions in the city of Caruaru.

Research hypothesis

How can deaf people travel independently to tourist attractions in Caruaru without the help of an interpreter?

Object of study

Accessible information system.

Scientific research methodology

This research is applied, as its results solve a real market problem. The approach of this research is qualitative as the focus is on the type of user response and not the quantity of responses. Semi-structured interviews will be carried out in order to gather the necessary information.

1- The universe of the deaf

For many years, deaf people were seen as disabled, abnormal, sick and incapable of participating in society and interacting (STROBEL, 2008). Unfortunately, deaf people have been analyzed through the lens of hearing impairment as a limitation, with the intention of normalizing and curing them. However, deaf people are not limited by their disability; they have their own culture and language, as will be explored in more detail in the sub-section "Deaf identity and culture" in this section.

Several deaf people have for years expressed this desire not to be seen as a person with a disability, as Laborrit (1994) states, "I refuse to be considered exceptional, handicapped. I'm not. I'm deaf. For me, sign language corresponds to my voice, my eyes are my ears. Honestly, I don't lack anything, it's society that makes me exceptional". With this statement, the author declares that she doesn't want to be treated as a person with a disability, but as a deaf person who is capable of performing any activity.

The names used for members of the deaf community are defined by the members in such a way as to make them less discriminatory and as faithful to reality as possible. According to Gesser (2009), the correct term for a person with a hearing deficit who uses sign language to communicate is "SURDO", remembering that it is not the correct use of the denominative term that eliminates social prejudices, "prejudices can be disguised even in speeches that claim to assume difference and diversity".

The term "deaf-mute", according to FENEIS[1] (2006), is an incorrect definition "because the fact that a person is deaf does not mean that they are mute". It's common for this confusion to occur, as only a small proportion of the deaf population can pronounce words correctly, but as stated above, being deaf doesn't mean you're mute, mute is another disability.

ANDRADE (2011) explains that:

Just as there are many factors that lead to deafness, there are also many types of hearing loss: conductive hearing loss: This means that the sound waves can't reach the inner ear completely, due to problems with the outer or middle ear; Sensory hearing loss, where the sound transmission apparatus is in its normal form, but there is some kind of alteration in the quality of the sound; Central hearing loss, a very rare type, which is why it is so difficult to define and conceptualize, is characterized by patients who supposedly have normal hearing but can't understand what is being said to them.; and Functional hearing loss, in which case the patient loses their hearing due to emotional or psychic motivations.

Finally, as (SKLIAR 1997:33 apud GESSER 2009,p46) argues, "the construction of identities does not depend on greater or lesser biological limitations, but on complex linguistic, historical, social and cultural relationships". Members of the deaf community accept themselves as they are, recognize their linguistic differences and adopt sign language as their first language.

However, there are different types of deaf identities, and within this diversity some hearing-impaired

---

1 National Federation for the Education and Integration of the Deaf

people do not identify with the deaf community and consequently wish not to be part of it (STROBEL, 2008).

1.1 Deaf identity and culture

The concept of culture is quite wide-ranging, as Nunes states: "culture, a term so loaded with diverse values that its role varies remarkably from one author to another and of which more than 250 definitions are listed" (RICOU; NUNES, 2005). There are several different ways of conceptualizing culture, each author relates it in the way that is most appropriate. In relation to deaf culture, what the authors agree on is the importance of the spatial-visual form of communication, where visual language is primordial for the development of culture.

Deaf people have their own cultural characteristics, and this culture "is visual, it translates visually" (QUADROS, 2002, p10). What characterizes deaf culture is the way in which deaf people understand the world and make it accessible and habitable, modifying it with their visual perceptions. This includes the language, deaf ideas, beliefs, customs and habits of these people. We can understand that deaf people share something that makes them a unit, language is the main factor that classifies this culture, where deaf individuals identify and complete each other in behavior, norms and values, as STROBEL (2008) and GESSER (2009) agree.

According to Hall (1997), the culture we have determines our way of being, explaining, seeing, interpreting and understanding the world we live in. Due to the absence of hearing, deaf people understand the world through their eyes. This characteristic of seeing and understanding everything visually gives rise to deaf culture, characterized by sign language, which is the way deaf people understand the world in which they live, through which they can express themselves and absorb knowledge.

1.2 LIBRAS - The Brazilian Sign Language

A major milestone in the early history of sign language was the Milan Congress of 1880, where scholars from various countries determined that sign language was detrimental to the learning of oral language and should therefore be banned. As a result of this determination, for over 100 years deaf people were subjected to the techniques of oralism[2] and consequently to exhaustive, repetitive and mechanical speech training. DE LACERDA (1998) states that after the Milan Congress "an era of tolerated coexistence in deaf education between spoken and sign language ends" and the deaf teacher, who was quite common in deaf schools, ceases to exist.

The researcher Skliar (1998:7) explains some historical facts:

---

2 Oralism: Spoken language is prioritized as a form of communication for deaf people and learning oral language is advocated as indispensable for the integral development of children (Trenche 1995).

For over a hundred years, practices have been driven by attempts at correction, normalization and institutional violence; special institutions that have been regulated both by charity and beneficence, and by the prevailing social culture that required the ability to control, separate and deny the existence of the deaf community, sign language, deaf identities and visual experiences, which determine the set of differences between deaf people and any other group of subjects.

Human beings are social beings and deaf people are not exempt from this statement. Nowadays, most deaf Brazilians use LIBRAS (Brazilian Sign Language) to communicate with each other and with listeners who know LIBRAS. Continuing on, let's look at what Gesser (2009, p12) points out: "the impulse of individuals to communicate is universal and, in the case of the deaf, this impulse is signaled".

Translating Portuguese into LIBRAS is essential for better inclusion of the deaf and reaffirmation of their culture.

Sign language is one of the main hallmarks of the identity of a deaf people, as it is one of the peculiarities of deaf culture, it is a form of communication that captures the visual experiences of deaf subjects, and it is this language that will lead the deaf to transmit and provide them with the acquisition of universal knowledge (STROBEL, 2008, p44).

For more than 100 years, deaf people have been limited in the use of sign language, which has also limited the linguistic development of the language for many years. From the 1950s onwards, studies began into the recognition of sign language. Scholars from this period include: the American William Stokoe (1965), the Brazilian hearing women: Lucinda Ferreira Brito(1986), Ronice Quadros(1995;2004), Tanya Felipe(2002) and Lodenir Karnopp(2004) and deaf Brazilians: Ana Regina e Souza Campello(2007) and Shirley Vilhalva(2007), with these scholars spaces were opening up for sign language.

There are currently laws that protect deaf people and guarantee them the rights they need for their health, education and social well-being. Parts of these laws are described below, BRAZIL. Law No. 10.436, OF APRIL 24, 2002, Published in the Official Gazette of the Union on April 24, 2002. This law provides for the recognition of the Brazilian Sign Language (LIBRAS) as a language used by deaf communities in Brazil of a visual-motor nature. It decrees that public authorities in general and public service concessionaires support the use and dissemination of the Brazilian Sign Language, as well as the appropriate treatment of hearing-impaired people. It also stipulates that the federal education system and the state, municipal and Federal District education systems must ensure that Special Education, Speech Therapy and Teaching courses at secondary and higher education levels include the teaching of the Brazilian Sign Language - Libras, as an integral part of the National Curriculum Parameters - PCNs, in accordance with current legislation. However, Libras will not be able to replace the written modality of the Portuguese language and makes other provisions.

Federal Law No. 5.626 considers and defines "a deaf person as one who, due to hearing loss, understands and interacts with the world through visual experiences, manifesting their culture mainly through the use of the Brazilian Sign Language - Libras". It also reinforces the items described in the previous law, defines how teachers will be trained to teach LIBRAS and makes other provisions.

It is important to understand the particular grammatical structure of LIBRAS, especially in order to carry out a comprehensible translation. Like Portuguese, sign language also has its own classification and structure, which is made up of smaller parts that have no meaning on their own. The American linguist William Stokoe was one of the scholars of sign language. He began his studies in 1960, describing the phonological and morphological levels of American Sign Language, the acronym is ASL, the linguist points out three parameters that make up sign language and named them: Hand configuration (CM), point of articulation (PA) and movement (M). These three parameters are shown in the figure below:

Figure 1 - Representation of the Stokoe parameters of the word certainty.

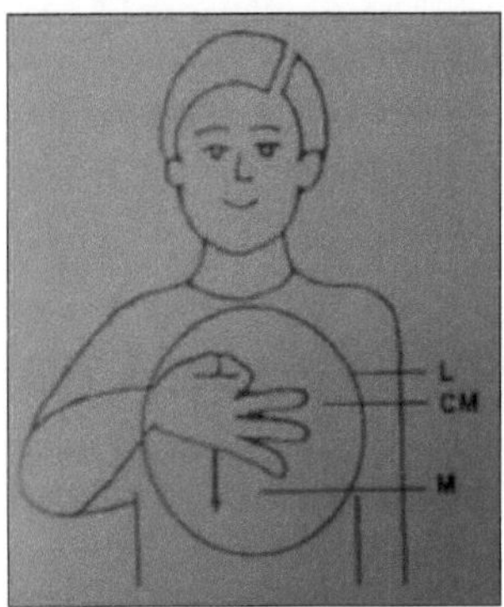

Source: Drawing adapted from Capovilla & Raphael (2004,p 194)

As shown in the figure, the hand configuration is the shape of the hand used to represent a given sign, the articulation point or location is the place where the sign will be executed, which can be in neutral space (not touching any part of the body) or touching some part of the body, the movement, as the name implies, is the movement that must be executed in order to understand a given sign. Just as in Portuguese if you change a letter in a word, you can completely change the meaning of the word, this also happens in LIBRAS if you change the hand configuration, the location or the movement of a sign, you change the whole meaning of the word.

We can cite the complementary studies of linguists: Robbin Battison (1974), Edward S. Klima & Ursulla Bellugi (1979), who entered the studies on ASL grammar, adding and describing an important parameter: palm orientation. According to Quadros and Karnopp (2004), the orientation parameter is the direction in which the palm of the hand points when we produce the sign. There are 6 hand orientation positions: up and down, in and out and sideways. Based on research into non-manual features (EKMAN, 1978; AARONS ET AL, 1992 apud FELIPE, 1997), we can talk about a fifth parameter: facial and body expressions. In this parameter, facial and body expression, movements of the body, face, head and eyes directly influence the correct understanding of the word.

The manual alphabet is used to spell out names, places, acronyms or words that don't yet have a sign. This resource plays a very important role in the interaction of deaf people, also known as digital spelling or typing. It can also be used to represent punctuation marks, such as commas, periods, question marks, mathematical signs and more. Some people who don't have in-depth knowledge of the subject believe that the manual alphabet is sign language in its entirety, Gesser says that to believe this is to "fixate on the idea that sign language is limited". (2009, p29). According to Gesser, "the manual alphabet is made up of 27 shapes, including the "ç". Each hand shape is equivalent to a letter of the Brazilian Portuguese alphabet." Below is an illustration of the signs equivalent to this alphabet:

Figure 2 - Manual alphabet

Source:http://escritadesinais.wordpress.com/2010/09/07/alfabeto-manual-ou-datilologia/

1.3 *Sign* writing

Sign writing is the graphic representation of sign language, but it is still not very widespread among the deaf community, according to Gesser (2009, p42) "like any language writing is a system of representation, an extremely sophisticated convention of reality, which is a set of second-order symbols". This definition fits sign language and the verbal languages we know.

As Strobel tells it, the deaf doctor Marianne Stumpf, together with other researchers, developed this research into the Sign writing system in Brazil. This system is now known in Brazil as ELS "Escrita em Lingua de sinais" (2008). These studies were very important for the development of written sign language in Brazil. There are currently ELS courses in some of Brazil's Federal Colleges, mainly in the literature/libras course. Below is an illustration of the written signs equivalent to the alphabet in Libras:

Figure 3 - Alphabet sign wririting

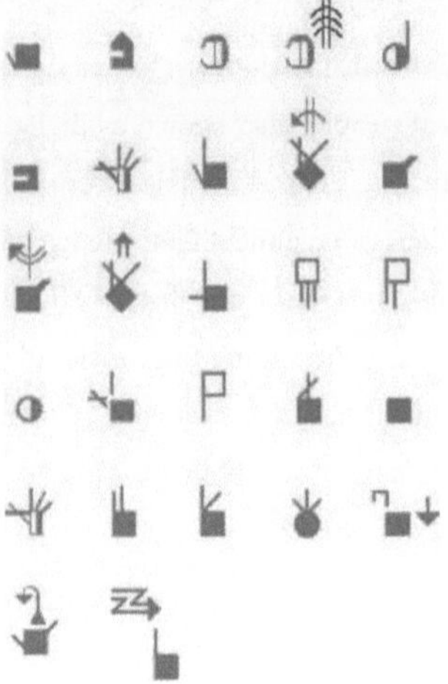

Source:http://escritadesinais.wordpress.com/2010/09/07/alfabeto-manual-ou-datilologia/

This type of sign writing, which was originally written by hand, can now be done using computer programs[3] . The system in Brazil is still in the experimentation phase, because the spelling is going through a process of standardization, each deaf person writes the "graphemes" differently in terms of detail, more in-depth studies are needed to understand the symbols and disseminate them in the deaf community (Gesser, 2009). For this reason, we chose not to use them in the construction of the application.

---

3 For more details go to http://www.signwriting.org/brazil/

2 - Tourism

Tourism is one of the oldest human activities, considering man's ability to explore, get to know, conquer and create relational spaces for trade, only in recent decades has it contributed "significantly to the economic, social and cultural development of a large number of countries, becoming a highly profitable business [...]" (ACERENZA, 2002, p. 13 apud SILVA, 2009). Cities that participate in tourism, whether for business or pleasure, have been encouraged to invest in improving roads, transportation, hotels and restaurants in order to cater for tourists and generate profits.

The writer Almeida (ibidem) states that tourism is one of the main economic activities nowadays, bringing with it income generation in the receiving region, socio-cultural development and consequently the well-being of tourists. As a result, tourism becomes a key factor in improving cities, benefiting both tourists and locals.

"Tourism "[...] has become a human right recognized by the Universal Declaration of Human Rights, affirming itself as a social necessity." (ALMEIDA, 2006). (2006) In other words, understanding the needs of human beings, such as culture, well-being, leisure, as a priority, before seeing human beings as consumers: a source of income. By satisfying the needs of the human being as a social being, the income generated in tourism will be a consequence.

That's why creating a space that meets the expectations of deaf tourists is essential, "[...] because it combines the economic aspect with a sense of pleasure, of welcome, of a space reserved for tourists to have their wishes, desires and needs met." (SILVA 2009). As a result, deaf tourists who are satisfied with the city will return more often and recommend it to other people, making this a cycle of income generation.

2.1 Tourism in Caruaru[4]

The city of Caruaru, 132 kilometers from Recife, in the Agreste region of Pernambuco, has many tourist attractions that are available all year round. It receives visitors from all over Brazil and even abroad, as happens during Holy Week and Sao Joao. As a result of the 30-day June festivities and popular events, Caruaru is recognized throughout Brazil. (PREFEITURA DE CARUARU, 2015)

As we have seen, the city of Caruaru has great cultural and artistic potential, and some academic studies demonstrate the city's potential to be considered a creative city in the future. According to Takako (2015) "creative cities is a term linked to the creative economy, which is based on cities that promote the integration, approximation and direct and indirect participation of citizens with local culture". Since the creation of something that facilitates this integration of citizens without restrictions

---

4 Most of the data on this topic was obtained from the Caruaru Culture Foundation at: https://www.caruaru.pe.gov.br/secretaria/fundacao-de-cultura-e-turismo-de-caruaru.

and respecting differences favors the city and its regional culture, the possibility of Caruaru being considered a creative city is getting closer.

Still according to Takako, information and communication technologies in these "creative cities bring together and attract a new audience, most of whom are unaware of the cultural richness that is present in the environment where they live, either through lack of interest or lack of dissemination...". In this context, deaf people are showing themselves to be this new audience that is being restricted from absorbing the local cultural wealth due to a lack of publicity that is understandable to them.

Tourist attractions in Caruaru

Below are the main fixed points of cultural tourism in Caruaru.

Figure 4 - Alto do Moura

Source: Caruaru City Hall[5]

Alto do Moura is located 7 km from the center of Caruaru. In this neighborhood, the saga of the Caruaru artisans began, with Mestre Vitalino as its main character. Today, the site represents one of the most significant centers of figurative arts in the Americas." (CARUARU, 2015).

Figure 5 - Mestre Vitalino house museum

Source: Caruaru City Hall

The Mestre Vitalino House-Museum is located in Alto do Moura and "was the residence where

---

5 Figures taken from the website : https://www.caruaru.pe.gov.br/pontos-turisticos

Caruaru's most famous artisan Mestre Vitalino lived during the last years of his life". The attraction of this place for tourists is the exhibition of the Master's works, household utensils and photographs belonging to the Vitalino family (idem).

Figure 6 - Zé cabloco clay museum

Source: Caruaru City Hall

"The Zé Caboclo Clay Museum is located in one of the annexes of the Tancredo Neves Cultural Space. It is present on the municipality's main tourist routes and is a showcase for regional culture." (CARUARU, 2015)

Figure 7- City Museum

Source: Caruaru City Hall

"Museu das cidades is where the old flour market used to be, on a corner of Rua Duque de Caxias, the City Museum houses old photos of Caruaru, highlighting the Feira when it was located in the center." (Idem).

Figure 8 - Vasconcelos Sobrinho Park and Severino Montenegro Municipal Environmental Park

Source: tvreplay [6]

The Vasconcelos Sobrinho Park and the Severino Montenegro Municipal Environmental Park are two of the city's main environmental parks. The Vasconcelos Sobrinho Park is located in Murici, in the rural area of the city. The Severino Montenegro Municipal Environmental Park "is located in the area of the old seedbed, this park has a sensory garden, a lake with a waterfall, an amphitheatre, toilets and parking" (CARUARU, 2015).

Figure 9- Cordel Museum

Source: Caruaru City Hall

The Cordel Museum exhibits traditional cordels, woodcut machines and Iinogravures. "The Cordel Museum, located at the Craft Fair, is a tribute to the Caruaru cordelist Olegârio Fernandes, who described the history of the man from the Northeast, especially from Caruaru, in a poetic way."

---

6 Figures taken from the website : http://www.tvreplay.com.br/jornalismo/caruaru-pe-horario-de-funcionamento- dos-parques-municipais-d durante-carnaval/

(CARUARU, 2015).

Figure 10 - José Condé House of Culture

Source: Caruaru City Hall

The José Condé House of Culture is located inside the Caruaru Fair. There are several temporary exhibitions in the Caruaru space, as well as fixed exhibitions such as [...] "a display of the Caruaru Fair with objects made of leather, clay, wood, straw and also a gallery of popular toys, with pieces of children's imagination produced at the Fair [...]" (CARUARU, 2015).

Figure 11 - Events park

Source: Caruaru City Hall

The event park is an "open area of 40,000 square meters, forming the complex where Sao Joao is held together with the Tancredo Neves Cultural Space, which functions as the city's convention center" [...] (SILVA 2009, p.20).

Figure 12 - Onildo Almeida Handicraft Fair

Source: Caruaru City Hall

The world-renowned handicraft fair is located in Parque 18 de Maio, with stalls selling handicrafts in clay, leather, straw, wood, handicrafts, hammocks and more (CARUARU, 2015).

Figure 13 - Caruaru Fair

Source: Caruaru City Hall

According to the Caruaru City Hall, the free fair recurs every week. Caruaru receives around 40,000 visitors a week. "The Caruaru Fair, which today represents one of the city's main tourist attractions, is considered one of the most important fairs in Brazil." (idem, 2015).

2.2 Tourism accessible to all

"It is important to stress that disability is not synonymous with illness, nor is it the inability to interact with society." (ALBUQUERQUE, 2012). People with disabilities have the capacity to carry out any activity.

The definition of accessibility according to ABNT (NBR 9050): It is the "Possibility and condition of reach, perception and understanding for the use with safety and autonomy of buildings, space, furniture, urban equipment and elements." It is therefore necessary to create means that enable people with disabilities to have free access to tourism, breaking down physical barriers as well as language barriers.

According to some Portuguese language dictionaries, the definition of accessibility is: "(from Latin: acessibilitate) 1. Ease of access, of obtaining.2. Ease in dealing with" (MODERNO DICIONARIO DA LÌNGUA PORTUGUESA - MICHAELIS 2000, p. 37); 1. Quality or character of being accessible. 2. easy to approach, deal with or obtain." (NOVO DICIONARIO DA LINGUA PORTUGUESA - AURÉLIO, p.22). Therefore, facilitating access to and obtaining culture through tourism means making it accessible. To make it understandable and to reinforce the guarantee of accessibility, laws have been passed, such as those described below:

Decree 5.296/2004:

Accessibility is related to providing conditions for the safe and autonomous use, total or assisted, of urban spaces, furniture and equipment, buildings, transport services and communication and information devices, systems and media, by people with disabilities or reduced mobility.

The above decree characterizes accessibility as a right for disabled citizens. Therefore, we can emphasize that the social duty to create means of access to environments and information for the disabled is more than reaffirmed.

Article 2 of the World Tourism Code of Ethics states:

Tourism activities must respect equality between men and women, and must tend to promote human rights and especially the particular rights of groups such as children, the elderly, the disabled, ethnic minorities and indigenous peoples (BOITEUX, 2003, p. 113). So that everyone has their human rights to leisure and culture respected.

In 2009, the Ministry of Tourism (Mtur) launched a booklet called "Accessible Tourism". The booklet consists of four volumes and contains information on the laws that guarantee accessibility rights for people with special needs. This booklet was of great importance for the dissemination of requirements, such as mobility for the disabled by means of: ramps (for wheelchair users), wider seats and access (for the obese), materials in Braille (for the visually impaired), among other facilities to make access to the environment safer and more comfortable (ANDRADE, 2011). We can say that initiatives such as the one described above are necessary to create measures that facilitate access for people with special needs to the most diverse environments. Human beings are different by nature, and disabled people in particular need their differences to be seen by society and means devised to facilitate access to basic needs, as in the case of tourism, culture and leisure.

3 - Information systems

We all deal with information systems on a daily basis, whether they are printed or digital. According to Davis (1985) apud Freire (2015), an information system is anything that contains information and has value for generating a decision. We can consider information systems to be elements that interact to achieve objectives, such as printed instruction manuals, displays and panels, signage systems, pictograms and symbols, warnings and so on. The system is defined as a set of elements or components that interact to achieve objectives, these components consist of inputs, transformations and outputs (*input* ⟶ **interface** → *output*)".

Complementing this, Freire (idem) defines that the user of an information system goes through three phases: perception, comprehension and decision. These phases occur in both printed and digital systems. The perception phase, which takes place in the perceptual system, consists of detecting the message, identifying and recognizing the system. The comprehension phase, which takes place in the cognitive system, uses short-term memory (STM) as well as long-term memory (LTM) and finally the decision-making phase, which takes place in both the cognitive and perceptual systems, involves making decisions and detecting ways of showing a response. In this process, which goes from understanding the information to the system's response, we must take into account all the ergonomic activity we can apply, in order to make the product more understandable and easier to use, thus avoiding errors in use and consequent frustration.

3.1 Digital information systems

Information systems are made up of the elements of digital interfaces that interact and generate results. "The interface of an interactive system comprises the entire portion of the system with which the user maintains physical contact (motor, perceptual or conceptual during the interaction)". Moran (1981) apud Silva & Barbosa (2010).

It is essential to understand how this relationship between the user and the system takes place. The authors Kim and Lee (2005) apud Padovanni et al (2013) developed a model with four stages of interaction that take place in digital systems: perception, navigation, execution and confirmation, which explains this interaction well. Below is a table that explains this interaction step by step.

Figure 14 - User activity table

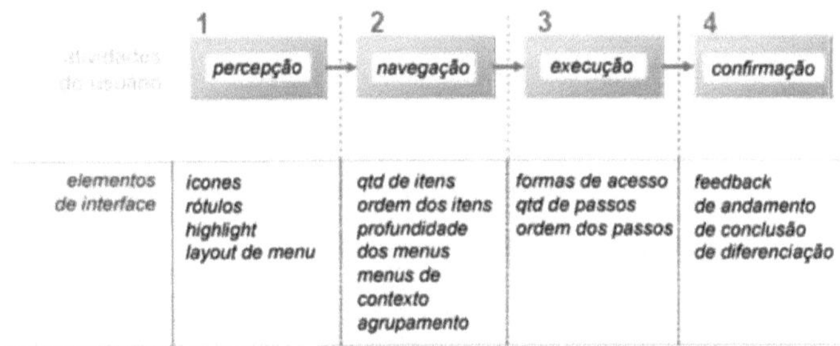

Source: Kim and Lee (2005) apud Padovanni et al (2013)

This whole process takes place in seconds subconsciously and is finally externalized. First the user perceives the graphical interface and all the elements belonging to it, during navigation he perceives the number of menus, intensives and the context of groupings, in the execution stage he chooses which action he is going to perform. Finally, in the confirmation stage, the user receives feedback, i.e. the system's response to the task performed.

3.2 Ergonomic recommendations for information systems

Information ergonomics is a discipline that helps in the understanding and creation of interfaces, as stated by Freire (2014) "Information ergonomics is the discipline that studies the interaction between humans and information systems". Several authors who write about information ergonomics reinforce the idea that the focus of the project should always be the user and their design needs.

For example, the authors Cybis et al. (2007) say that the aim of ergonomics "is to ensure that systems and devices are adapted to the way users think, behave and work and thus provide usability". Projects must be based on knowing which users they are, what their needs are and how they interact in order to design a system that is ergonomic to the task. Ergonomics supports the organization of information in such a way that the user can better understand what is happening in this interaction, and ultimately be able to carry out the proposed task.

And as Nielsen (1993) apud Silva & Barbosa (2010) reaffirms "Usability is related to the ease of learning and using the interface, as well as the satisfaction resulting from this use." Interfaces that use ergonomic principles in their design tend to make the user's experience with the interface easier. Sharp et al (2007) apud Silva & Barbosa (2010) add that "sometimes this quality related to the user's feelings is called user experience". The goal of any project should be to facilitate the user's understanding by making the experience as pleasant and frustrating as possible.

In this respect, Silva & Barbosa (2010) state that "The user interface determines the possible interaction processes, as it determines what the user can say or do, in what way and in what order". It is necessary to understand what each part of the interface is communicating to the user and how they understand this message.

In order to find out who the users are and what their needs are, tests should be carried out with predetermined users to observe how they interact with the prototype under controlled conditions, to perform a task with defined objectives in a usage scenario (Agner, 2006). Understanding the user's wishes is fundamental to the success of the project. Some features even unconsciously guide users on how to interact correctly with the system, and we can describe them as principles for digital interfaces. Within these principles there are the affordances that "correspond to the set of characteristics of an object capable of revealing to its users the operations and manipulations they can do with it" defines Norman (1988) apud Silva & Barbosa (2010). It's important to note that some care must be taken to avoid generating false affordances. As Lupton (2014) exemplifies, when a developer uses a text box or command button just to display a message, it can confuse the user into imagining that the box is clickable without it having this functionality and, consequently, generate frustration.

As described above, it is important to note that errors can occur in small details such as a button or link. Krug (2005) points out that links and buttons should be obvious, you shouldn't spend a millisecond thinking about whether something should be clicked or not. In order for a button or link to really give the right impression of what it is, buttons should have rounded corners as they suggest size and thus easily associated with buttons, underlined words and/or color indicates that by clicking on the text, the user will be taken to another screen (Lupton 2014). By using these devices, errors in use will be avoided.

Lupton (idem) describes a physical characteristic that must be taken into account when it comes to sizes and proportions, as almost all interactions with the screen on mobile devices occur with the finger, for the user to be able to click accurately they need clickable items of at least 50 px, subtle changes in the object when the mouse passes over it indicate that that element generates interaction. According to Krug (2005), the information should be very obvious and clear to understand, the names to be used should be well chosen, the appearance, organization and small amount of text should be well placed, the user should not spend too much time thinking about what to do, this process should be intuitive.

Below we describe some of the requirements that apply to mobile design and that will be followed in the realization of this digital interface project. It all starts here at this stage, planning the site and navigation map. This part can also be called the system's information architecture and consists of establishing the main screens and navigation routes. This stage is what we call a "wireframe" or grid. A wireframe is a low-fidelity representation of what the system's interface will contain. It should be like a "board with axes" that defines areas of concentration for similar information, according to FREIRE (2015). As in the example below:

Figure 15 - Wireframe

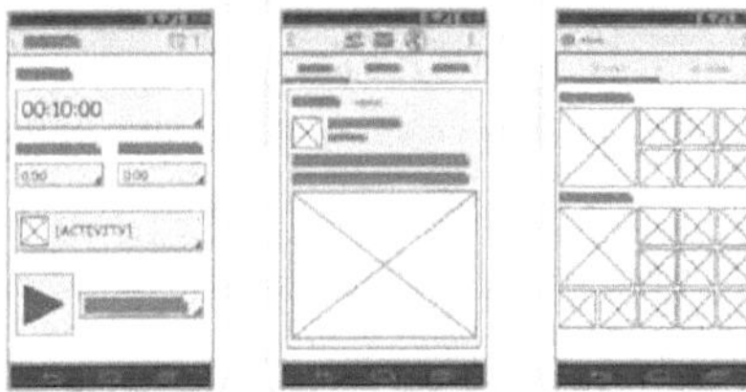

Source yeeply.com accessed on 13/12/2015

Visual features help to create a visual hierarchy that creates clarity of understanding, such as bold, colors and location. Similar items should be grouped together, either in a visually similar way or in a defined area.

Shneiderman (2004) apud Cybis (2007) defined eight rules that are called golden rules, which take into account items that should not be missing in any digital interface project. (1) Consistency, because the repetition of patterns is important, such as the layout of colors, typology, menus and basic layout. Sequences of actions should be repeated in order to fix the paths to be followed in the user's mind. (2) If necessary, there can be shortcuts for the more experienced to use, if they wish, in order to shorten the path to be followed. (3) Include informative feedback in the system, to generate responses to user actions. Lack of feedback or its delay can give the user the wrong impression that the system is failing, and they may take action that disrupts the processes in progress. (4) Make it clear when the dialogue ends. Every project should have a logical sequence and a precise ending, which gives the user a sense of security. (5) Human errors should also be anticipated in order to avoid them. As Freire (2014) reaffirms, human errors must be prevented. If errors persist during use, they are characterized as design errors, not system errors. The project must be designed to make it impossible (exclusionary design) or at least difficult (prevention design) to carry out wrong actions and to minimize the consequences of errors ("fail-safe" design). (6) Allowing the cancellation of actions, this means that the user must have the option of returning to the initial stage at any time, giving them a sense of security. (7) Control is the user's, this control should always be prioritized, the user feels safer knowing that they are in control of the situation.

(8) The next rule prioritizes the reduction of the working memory load, defining that not too much information is used that requires the user to use a lot of memory, what is possible must be visible or easy for the user to find.

And finally, as we've seen before, know the user, systems that don't consider the user as a central element alienate users, the success of the project depends on clarity and simplicity.

4 - Scientific methodology

In the construction of the tourism application for the municipality of Caruaru, we will use the theoretical framework as a basis for construction. This foundation includes the definition of the deaf community, as well as tourism in the city, emphasizing the need to include accessible tourism and, finally, information system theories. This work was based on bibliographic research, books, websites and scientific articles. In this research, it was decided to examine an existing tourism application and carry out tests with deaf people in order to identify its accessibility shortcomings.

This research is classified as applied research because it is characterized by its practical interest, i.e. that the results are applied or used immediately to solve the proposed problem. It solves a real problem and is applicable to the market.

The approach is qualitative because, during the tests of the chosen application "Guia de Caruaru", a semi-structured interview takes place. The stages of this interview are: Hand over a smartphone with the application already installed and open, and ask the user to carry out the four pre-determined tasks within 10 minutes, during which time the interviewer will analyze whether or not the interviewee has carried out the activity and answer the questionnaire. The interviewer will also evaluate any additional observations made by the user while using the application.

The procedural method is functionalist. This functionalist method is interpretive, and involves "analyzing the main differentiations of functions that must exist in a small isolated group in order for it to survive; investigating the function of uses and customs in ensuring the cultural identity of a group" (Lakatos, 1981:34). Therefore, we will draw conclusions from interpreting the lifestyle of deaf society with the intention of guaranteeing the cultural identity of this group.

Studies in the field of Digital Design have evolved over the last 50 years. However, there is a sub-area of digital design that involves several other areas and whose study has made this research multidisciplinary: it is the study of mobile applications for people with hearing limitations. One could only start from the area of usability or accessibility, but for this audience, there are particularities that also involve Information and Interaction Design.

This monograph could also have been based on research into UX - User Experience - and other sub-areas, but it was the decision of the researcher and her supervisor to delimit her research focus based on bibliographies that guide methods already consolidated in the field of Information Design, such as Garret's method (2003). If it were possible to have more time to study, as in the case of master's and doctoral degrees, other complementary methods would certainly be applied to the same study.

That said, the reference is a model for developing, analyzing and evaluating digital systems, with a focus on WEB design and other systems, such as software, etc. For this research, the aim was to develop a mobile application that would provide a tourist map of the city of Caruaru and that would be aimed at people who are deaf or have some form of hearing loss. Focusing on this audience, here is the description of the study.

Firstly, a semi-structured interview was carried out, based on the guidelines of Marcone and Lakatos (1998), where the researcher approached and interviewed a group of deaf people from a particular community/NGO in the city of Caruaru. The questions were answered on the basis of whether or not they had carried out the tasks proposed in a particular application that does not have accessibility and additional observations that the users pointed out.

The interview can be found in the appendices to this monograph (on page 59), but in summary, it contained four questions aimed at investigating factors that interfere with the use of a particular mobile application. We can see that the interview only has four questions because, as stated above, the focus of the research is qualitative and the aim of these questions is to visualize where the difficulties are in using the application.

Based on this interview, everything the interviewees said became a database for the development of a prototype mobile application containing a tourist map of Caruaru for this target audience. In this way, the interpretation of this data, which were the answers from the interviews, became the design requirements for Garret's (2003) method to be applied. Therefore, the answers were guidelines.

Garret's method (2003) will be explained later in this methodology section, but it must be said that each stage of its application was aimed at this particular target audience.

This is because when designing for non-disabled people, the aim is to achieve usability (or ease of use) that includes the use of sound as a system feedback tool. However, in the case of deaf people, the priority is VISUAL AND TATILE.

The following is a description of Garret's method and its project stages for digital design, as well as a description of how it was applied to this study, as already mentioned. Since this is a prototype of an application, final interfaces were developed in prototype format and had to be "tested" in a simulated way.

Garret's method (idem) is divided into 5 stages: Strategy, scope, structure, skeleton and surface. In the diagram below, Garret highlights the surface in the foreground, as it is the first thing the user sees, but in order to design we must follow the opposite path.

Figure 16 - Garret's Methodological Diagram

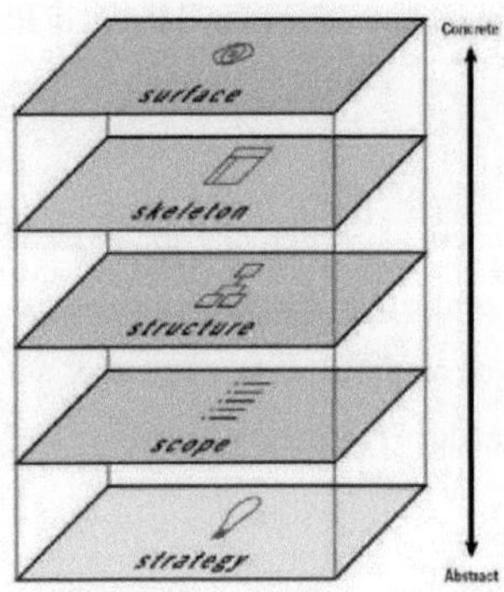

Source: Garrett, 2003

In the strategy phase, Garret (ibid.) states that the needs and objectives must be clear. To this end, the user's needs were analyzed through research, as well as the application's objectives and finally the strategy to be adopted. The research was carried out following the basic steps that Unger (2009) describes, according to which 5 steps are required: defining the primary user groups, planning user involvement, conducting the research, validating the group definitions and creating user requests.

In the sequence, Garret defines the scoping phase, in which we determine what to include, such as the specific content needed and the functionalities. The structural phase involves interaction design and information architecture, in this stage we define what is essential and how it will be included, we organize, divide and categorize.

According to Garret (2003, p. 108) the next phase, the skeleton, is where the function creates a format, the content takes shape and interacts through buttons, images and texts, proposing that "a successful interface is one in which the user immediately perceives what is most important". In the use of pictograms, according to Schiavenin (2015), the only thing needed to interpret the pictogram is perception: the sight of the pictogram makes us understand the information, regardless of the language the person speaks."

The surface plan is like the makeup of the product's skeleton, so it's important to enhance the senses (Garret 2003 p, 134;135). There are a few points that should be evaluated: Color, contrast, typography, grid and consistency. According to (Pavelecine, 2013), colors can be used to facilitate understanding and communicate an idea. The color to be used must be chosen carefully so as not to convey the wrong message. For Munari (2006, p. 339), quoted by Pavelecine (2013, p.27) "contrast is a very old rule of visual communication, which is enhanced and intensified by two forms of opposite nature".

Figure 17 - Readability ranking by contrast

Source: http://xtec.us/sign-tips.php. (Accessed on 15/12/2015)

According to Gomes Filho (2009, p. 65), ergonomically, contrast "provides better visibility, invisibility and visual acuity for information systems, as well as for coding chromatic signs and drawing attention to operating devices". The use of contrast is a tool to make the operating system more attractive and interesting for the user. When the product doesn't have this contrast, it risks becoming tedious, as it doesn't attract the user's attention.

Typography is an important part of the project, there are countless typographies available on the web for free use, some important points that we must evaluate when choosing typography, which are: Legibility, flexibility, elegance, readability, charisma and adaptability, however, these judgments are more subjective than scientific. It is therefore important to evaluate typography in the context in which it will be included, considering content, intentions and personal preferences (Lupton, 2014).

The grid is what we might call a wireframe that represents the structure and skeleton stages of Garret's methodology. The wireframe refers to the schematic of the page or screen design, which uses simplified elements to represent the basic content that the screen has (Idem).

The consistency of the navigation indicates the planned and coherent paths that the user can follow through the content (Lupton, 2014). This concludes with the construction of the path to be followed so that the user arrives at the desired information in the most logical and simple way possible.

5 - Data obtained

According to Unger (2009), it is necessary to prioritize the attributes "that seem to have the greatest impact on why and how a potential user would use your site or application". In order to understand which attributes the deaf community prioritizes, questionnaires were carried out.

The questionnaire was administered to 10 members of the deaf community from various age groups ranging from 14 to 56. Researcher Nielsen (2001) apud Agner (2006) argued that "with just five users it is possible to identify around 75% of critical interface problems". With this in mind, the number of participants was 10, because for the purposes of this research, the qualitative value outweighs the quantitative.

All members of the survey use smartphones on a daily basis. The interviewees were subjected to the use of a tourist app called "Guia de Caruaru", which does not have any kind of accessibility; they had to perform predetermined tasks. Below are the screenshots of the application used:

Figure 18 - First screen of the analyzed application

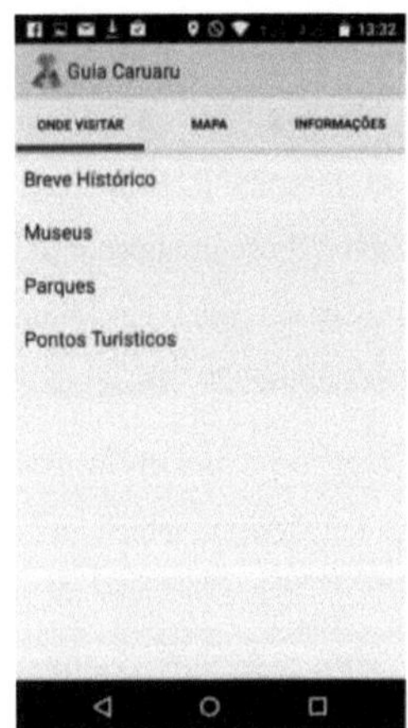

Source: Guia Caruaru.

These are the options that appear on the first screen when you open the application.

Figure 19 - Second screen of the analyzed application

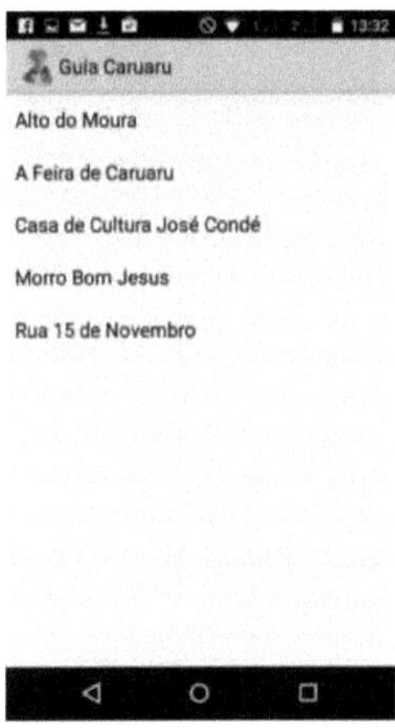

Source: Guia Caruaru.

This screen shows the names of the city's tourist attractions.

Figure 20 - Third screen of the analyzed application

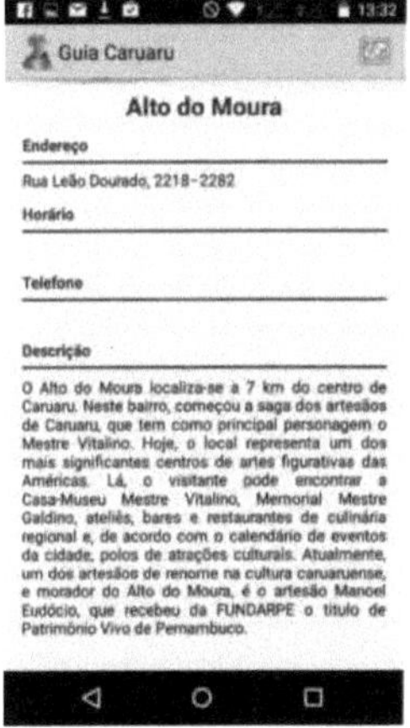

Source: Guia Caruaru.

This screen appears right after the user has chosen the Alto do Moura tourist attraction. It shows the address information and a description of the place.

Figure 21 - Fourth screen of the analyzed application

Source: Guia Caruaru.

This screen is where a brief history of the city is presented in running text.

The questionnaire was answered by the interviewer, according to whether or not a certain task had been carried out, with the help of a LIBRAS interpreter. Below are the results of the survey:

Graph 1

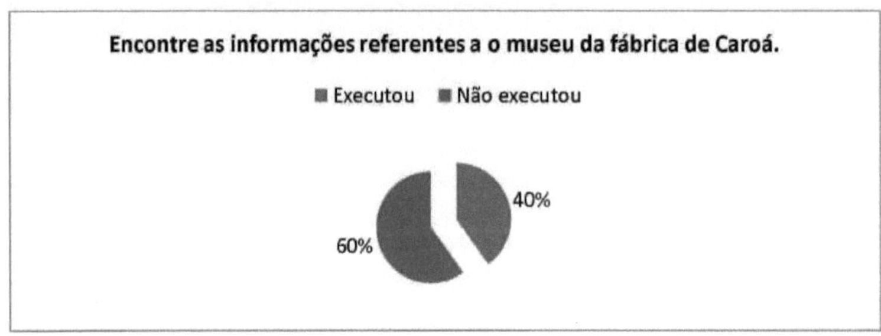

Source: author

Graph 2

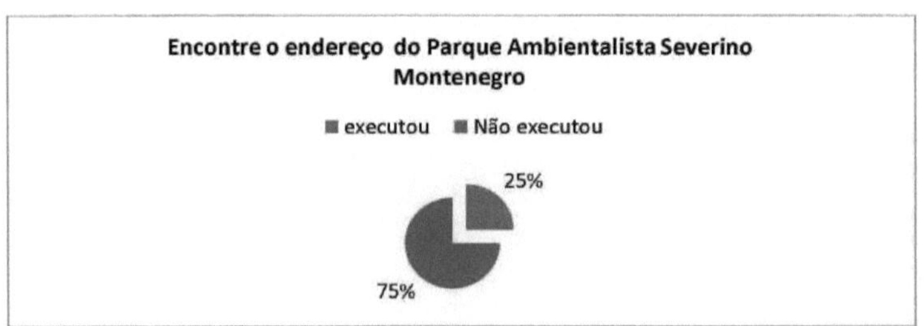

Source: author

Graph 3

Source: author

Graph 4

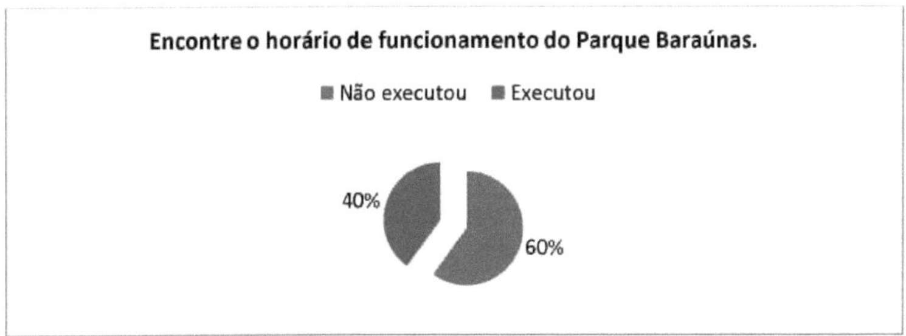

Source: author

All the users evaluated use smartphones on a daily basis. When analyzing the information collected, most of the interviewees were unable to correctly understand the meaning of the words, which took a long time to find the location requested by trial and error. (Of those who were unable to find the location requested, subsequent attempts were disregarded, because if they were successful, it was not by understanding but by trial and error). On screens with long texts, such as the one described in graph 3, the number of people who managed to understand what was written in the text was much lower.

6 - Data analysis and results

Based on the interviewees' responses and the non-verbal responses perceived by the interviewer, our target audience's priority is to use applications that use LIBRAS in their communication, replacing written words as much as possible. This directly influences and encourages the use of the application to the detriment of others available that do not have this differential, among other attributes that we will discuss below.

Navigation flowchart

Below you can see the navigation flowchart created as a result of this phase together with the previous ones. The result is a light and simple flowchart:

Figure 22 - Example of a navigation flowchart

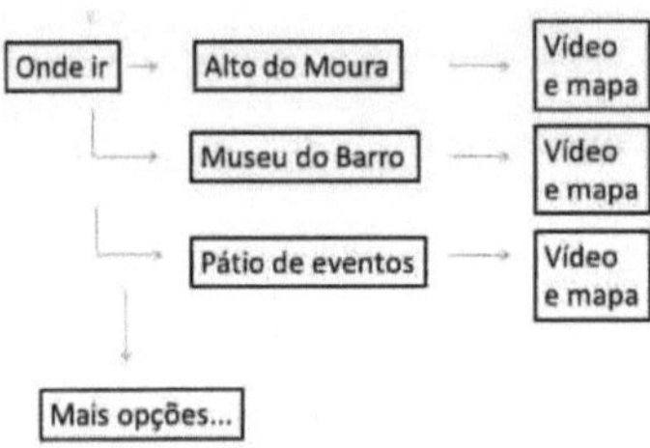

Source: Author

Videos

Facilitating independent travel is the main need for the application and the aim is to make it possible to understand through LIBRAS videos among other visual options such as maps, menus and pictograms. The videos in LIBRAS explained the transport options available for the chosen destination, and the interpretation into LIBRAS was done using an application called "Hand Talk" in which the application is fed with words in Portuguese, voice or photo. The image of the app is below.

Figure 23 - Images of the Hand Talk application

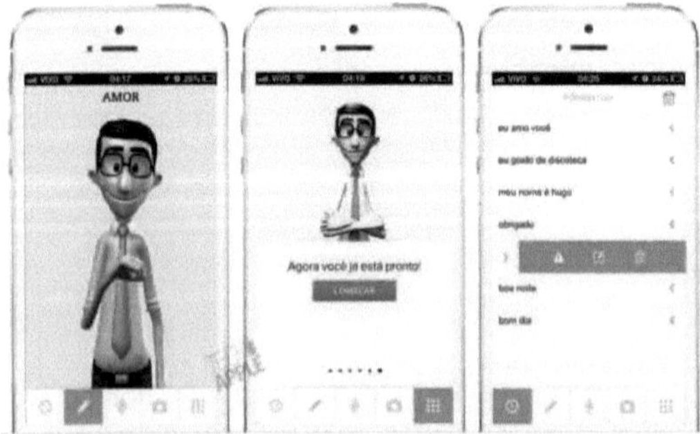

Source: Tech Apple

However, the sentences to be inserted do not follow the structure of the Portuguese language, so it is necessary to adapt the words to the structure of LIBRAS in order for the translation to be efficient. In relation to this structure, Nascimento (2008) apud Pereira (2010) explains that in LIBRAS:

there are no articles, not all the stative verbs there are in Portuguese and there are few connectors (prepositions and conjunctions). And the connectors that do exist don't have the plasticity of some of their Portuguese equivalents. In addition, the syntax of LIBRAS is of the spatial type, since the signs (equivalent to words in oral-auditory languages) constitute the sentences in the discursive space that extends from the head to the hips. All personal pronouns are represented in LIBRAS using the same resource: pointing to the referent or to an agreed place for that referent. Depending on the situational context and the utterance produced, the same sign can mean 'I' or 'me', for example. These are just some of the specificities of their mode of expression that contribute to deaf people having interactional difficulties with listeners.

To generate a comparative example, let's use the following sentence in the Portuguese grammatical structure: Alto do Moura is located 7 km from the center of Caruaru. You can go there by motorcycle taxi, taxi or bus. Below is an example of how this sentence should be translated. It is therefore necessary to have prior knowledge of how the grammatical structure of LIBRAS works in order to feed information into the videos of the tourist app:

Figura 24   - Hand Talk Translation

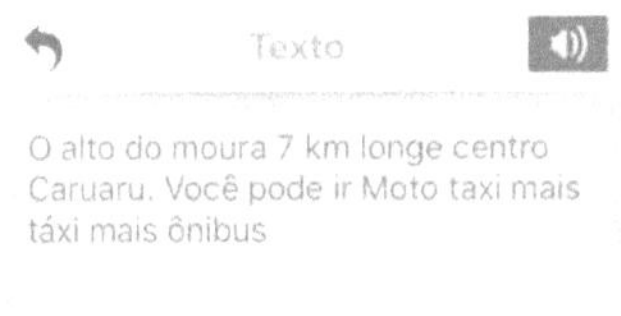

Source: Author (2015)

Initial Prototype

We used a website called "how" to create applications in order to create a high-fidelity prototype, as shown in the example below. The navigation is clear, simple and efficient. This way the user will know where to click to receive the information or perform the action they need, but this is not yet the final prototype, as it was not possible to include all the necessary requirements in this prototype, as it is a site that already has pre-determined templates, which can hardly be changed.

Figura 25   **- Home**

Source: 2015 Author's own

Maps

The maps used will be in the "Google maps" standard and will define the current GPS location to create a route to the destination according to the transportation to be used. If the user is not in Caruaru and wants to make a simulation, it is also possible to enter the desired departure location. Below is an example:

Figure 26 - Map

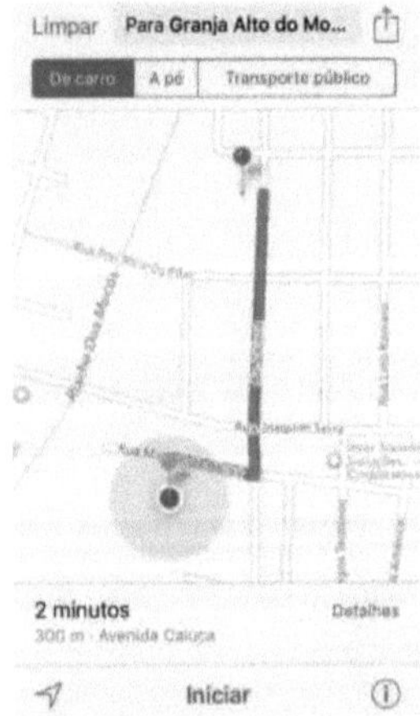

Source - Google maps

According to Freire (2015), some users find it difficult to understand the context of a two-dimensional map. However, this example map is interactive and can be navigated in 3D.

Menus

For the options menus, we used words that are easy to understand, such as: Where to go, where to eat, where to stay, instead of larger, complex words that could make it difficult to understand, making interactions quick and simple. As Cybis (2007) explained earlier, the menu can minimize the tasks to be carried out by the user if it provides quick access to the most frequently used options. The menu is a good option for use in mobile applications, instead of typing for searches on small screens should only be used as a last resort, the user should not spend too much time typing what they want, the ideal is if possible to have the options available in menus. We can reaffirm that menus are the best option, taking into account that, as we saw in the survey, our target audience has few typing skills, meaning that typing in the names of places for the purpose of searching would be complicated and would lead to several search failures.

Typography

As seen above, typography is an important part of the project. In order to choose the typeface, the following criteria were evaluated: legibility, flexibility, elegance, readability, charisma, adaptability according to the context in which it will be inserted, considering the content it will be part of and its intentions. According to Cybis (2007), sans-serif fonts look lighter, but are difficult to read in long texts; for long texts, serif fonts should be used. Therefore, the typeface to be chosen needs to be legible, but it doesn't necessarily need to read well in long texts, as long texts don't exist in the application.

Pictograms

Pictograms are easy to understand, as they are not very detailed, have a maximum of two colors and are represented by signs that are common. (Araùjo, 2014).The pictograms will act as adjuncts that, together with the words, will facilitate understanding, and some pictograms were chosen from the "I love Caruaru" collection by designer Otàvio Henrique. The illustrations created in this collection represent the city's most iconic elements, places and buildings (Gomes, 2015).

Figure 27 - "I love Caruaru" collection by Ótavio Henrique

Source: Gomes (2015)

Pictograms are images produced "that refer, however remotely, to the appearance or structure of something real or imagined" Lima (2009). Other pictograms will be used, for resources other than tourist attractions, as adjuncts; these will be the usual pictograms that are easy to assimilate.

Color

The color blue was chosen because it is the nationally representative color of the deaf community according to Dr. Paddy Ladd (deaf) and is used in a blue ribbon tie as a symbol in the celebrations of the date in September. Fraser (2012) explains that "[...] blue - the color of the sky and the sea, vast expanses that offer a perception of freedom and perspective - calms people". However, the author also points out that it can be considered a "cold" and even lonely color. Since the interpretation of this color depends a lot on the context, we will also insert the color yellow, considered a "warm color" that will generate contrast and hierarchy, the color yellow will be applied to the points that we want to highlight in the application, those that should get the most attention from the user.

Figure 28 - Colors used

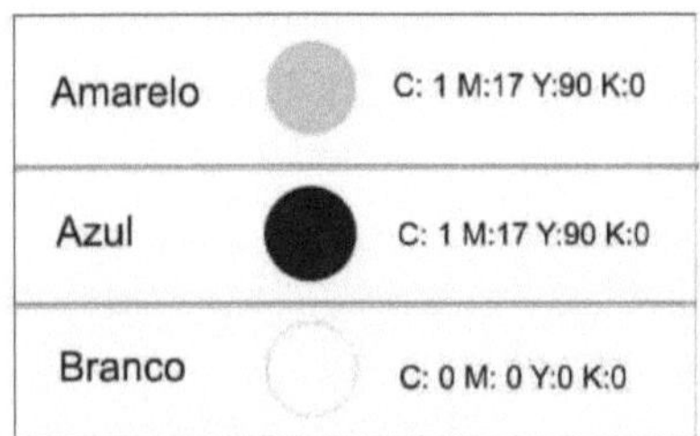

Source: 2016 Own author

Final prototype

All the requirements studied above were applied to the layout of the final prototype. Below is a drawing of the home screen, which will be the first to appear as soon as it is opened. The colors chosen for the application, orange and blue, have been applied to it. The layout of the icons and texts on the screen was designed along the standard diagonal line, from left to right and downwards.

Figure 29 - First screen of the final prototype

Source:2016 Author's own

This second screen has the name of the application highlighted at the top and a menu with three easy-to-associate options in boxes with rounded edges for easy assimilation with clickable buttons, If the user touches the button, it changes color and vibrates, enhancing the senses of sight and touch. Understanding what you will find by clicking on each box is made simple by the fact that the words are short and commonly used, along with the use of pictograms that act as a complement.

Figure 30 - Second screen of the final prototype

Source:2016 Author's own

Once the user has clicked on the "where to go" option, they will be taken to this third screen, where at the top there is a back button allowing the user to return to the previous screen, giving them a sense of autonomy. Below is the name of the page where the user is "Where to go". Below is the menu in the same pattern as the second screen, in order to create standardization and similarity on the screens. In the bottom corner there are the same three options as on the second screen; "where to go", "where to eat" and "where to stay", these options are available on this and the next page and also generate autonomy, generating a shortcut that can be used at any time which also highlights which page the user is on, according to image.

Figure 31 - Third screen of the final prototype

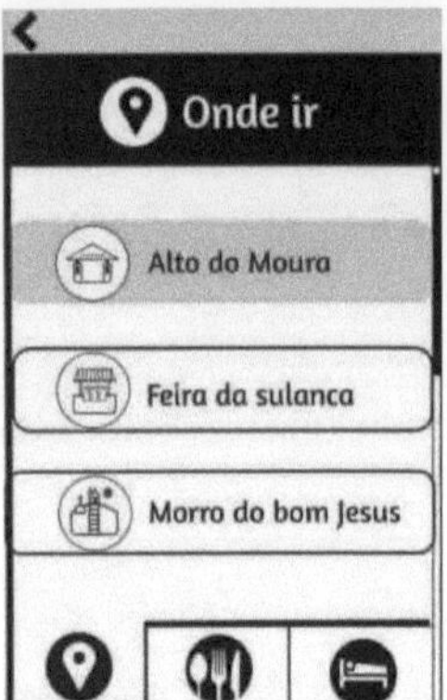

Source:2016 Author's own

The fourth screen appears after the user clicks on the chosen destination, which in this case is Alto do Moura, the back arrow appears again, the name of the place at the top of the page following the same pattern as the previous one, just below the video and map boxes in which the user can click and turn the screen horizontally to view it in a larger size, as shown in the image below:

Figure 32 - Fourth screen of the final prototype

Source:2016 Author's own

Figure 33 - Fifth screen of the final prototype

Source:2016 Author's own

Conclusion

After a long study, we achieved our research objectives, which were to develop a prototype of a tourist app for deaf people. The aim of this application is that, with its use, deaf people can have the independence to move around the city, visiting tourist attractions and using only a smartphone, where without much difficulty and easy handling the interested party can obtain all the information they need, in LIBRAS, such as: location, distance, means of transport and so on.

In order to achieve these objectives, we surveyed authors from various fields and relied on the collaboration of the deaf themselves in questionnaires, tests and simulations. In these questionnaires we detected what the design requirements of this community are for the designed product. In order to apply these questionnaires, we had the help of a LIBRAS interpreter, whose presence helped us to better understand the answers given by the deaf. As a result of the questionnaires, we can affirm that the Brazilian Sign Language (LIBRAS) enables better transmission and understanding of information, as well as other requirements.

The creation methodology used in this project was Garret's. As we applied the methodology, we felt that it was very complete and covered all the stages of the creation process. As adjuncts to this methodology, we used authors who added complementary knowledge.

We believe that with this device the deaf community will feel honored, since until now the deaf have depended almost entirely on an interpreter, which is not always possible. We know that deaf people are intelligent people, proof of this are the deaf professionals in the most diverse areas of activity, showing all their cognitive capacity and altruism and therefore no longer accept being discriminated against, as happened years and years ago, in a mediocre and hypocritical society, the deaf were considered a sub-race and freaks of nature, thanks to a lot of struggle by scholars and the deaf community, today we can say that society has evolved a lot.

For all these reasons, the future application created as a result of this prototype aims to make these people's visits more enjoyable, providing them with a better experience of tourism. And because of the good impression, when they return to their cities of origin they will become promoters of these benefits found in our city. Not only will they visit the city again, but they will also bring other people with the same needs. And we, as the receiving city, will be called a more humane and welcoming city. It is clear that further research on this subject is extremely important.

References

The importance of prototyping in mobile app development. Available at:

https://pt.yeeply.com/blog/a-importancia-do-prototipo-no-desenvolvimento-de-app-moveis/

Accessed on: Dec. 13, 2015.

ALBUQUERQUE, Judithe. Accessibility in tourism. **Natal: UFRN, 2012.ALMEIDA, Wolney. The deaf community and socially responsible tourism: a look at** differences. **Caxias do Sul: UCS, 2006.**

ARAUJO, Caio. Infographics by infographics: A methodological approach. **Volta** Redonda: Centro universitàrio de volta redonda, 2014.

AGNER, Luiz. **Ergodesign and information architecture. Rio de Janeiro**. Ed. Quartet. 2006.

AZEVEDO, Israel Belo de. **The pleasure of scientific production.** 7. ed. Piracicaba: UNIMEP, 1999. 208p.

BARBOSA, Simone Diniz Junqueira; SILVA, Bruno Santana. **Human-computer interaction.** Rio de Janeiro. Elsevier. 2010.

BOITEUX, B. **Legislaçao de turismo.** Topics of law applied to tourism. 2. ed. Rio de Janeiro: Campus, 2003.

BRAZIL. Decree 5296, of March 3, 2006. Regulates Laws No. 10.048, of November 8, 2000, which gives priority service to the people it specifies, and No. 10.098, of December 19, 2000, which establishes general rules and basic criteria for the promotion of accessibility. Diàrio Oficial [da] Repùblica Federativa do Brasil, Brasilia, DF, 2 dez. 2004. Available at: <http://www.bengalalegal.com/d5296>. Accessed on: August 12, 2014.

CANCLINI, Nestor Garcia. *Hybrid Cultures:* **Strategies for Entering and Exiting Modernity**. Sao Paulo. Edusp: 2000.

CYBIS, Walter. **Ergonomics and usability**. Sao Paulo: Ed Novatec, 2007.

Chocoladesign. **Signage - study and use of pictograms**. Available at: < http://chocoladesign.com/sinalizacao-estudo-e-uso-de-pictogramas/>. Accessed on: December 27, 2015.

NATIONAL FEDERATION FOR THE EDUCATION AND INTEGRATION OF THE DEAF. Available at: < http://www.feneis.com.br/Libras/index.shtml >. Accessed on: 12 August 2014

FELIPE, T.A. **O Signo Gestual-Visual e sua Estrutura Frasai na Lingua dos Sinais dos Centros**

Urbanos Brasileiros. Dissertation (Master's Degree) - Federal University of Pernambuco, Recife, 1988.

FRASER, Tom. **The essentials of color in design**. Sao Paulo: Editora Senac Sao Paulo, 2012.

FREIRE, Luciana. **Informational ergonomics: Master's classes.** Aug 01-14, 2014. 20 p. Class notes.

FREIRE. Luciana. **Informational ergonomics: Classroom notes UFPE - PE** . September 25, 2015. Classroom notes.

GESSER, Audrei. **Libras?: Que lingua é essa?: crenças e preconceitos em torno da lingua de sinais e da realidade surda** - Sao Paulo: Paràbola editorial, 2009.

GOMES, O. H. **icones_Caruaru** [personal message]. Message received by <iaracassia93@gmail.com> on 29 Nov. 2015

GOMES, Filho, J. **Gestalt do objeto: Sistema de leitura visual da forma.** Sao Paulo: Escritura editora, 2009.

HALL, Stuart. **The centrality of culture: notes on the cultural revolutions of our time.** In: Revista educaçao e realidade: cultura, media e educaçao. V. 22n. 3 jul.-dec. 1997.

KRUG, Steve. **Don't make me think.** 2nd ed. Altas books. 2008.

LIMA, Ricardo Cunha. **Analysis of Journalistic Infographics**. Master's dissertation. Rio de Janeiro: 2009.

LUPTON, Elen. **Types on Screen.** Ed. Gustavo. 2015.

MARCONI, Marina de Andrade; LAKATOS, Eva Maria. **Metodologia Cientifica** 5th Edition Sao Paulo: Editora atlas. 2003.

MUNARI, B. Design and visual communication. Contribution to a didactic methodology. Sao Paulo. Martins Fontes, 2006.

PADOVANI, Stephania. **Handout to accompany the course module.** Specialization Course in Ergonomics, Federal University of Amazonas, 2004.

PAVELECINE, Maiquel. **Proposal for a graphical interface for an event management system,** Porto Alegre, 2013

MUNICIPAL MUNICIPAL DECARUARU. Available at: < http://www.surdosol.com.br/programacao-do-sao-joao-em-caruaru-conta-com-interpreting-in-libras/>. Accessed on : 26 of Sep. 2015.

PEREIRA, Laerte Leonaldo ; NASCIMENTO, Glàucia Renata P. **Reading and comprehension of texts by deaf online ead students: Limits and possibilities.** Anais Eletrônicos, v. 2010, p. 110, 2010.

QUADROS, Ronice Muller; KARNOPP, Lonedir Becker. **Brazilian Sign Language - linguistic studies.** Porto Alegre: Artmed, 2004.

RICOU, Miguel; NUNES, **Rui. The deaf community: What future?** Text of a conference given by the Department of Bioethics and Medical Ethics of the Faculty of Medicine of the University of Porto at the seminar organized by AS Porto on 5 May 2001. Available at http://www.feneis.org.br/libras/portugal/comunidade_futuro.htm. Accessed on: May 3, 2005.

SKLIAR, Carlos. *A surdez:* **um olhar sobre as diferenças**. 2ª ed. Rio de Janeiro: Vozes, 1999.

SILVA, Bruno Santana ; BARBOSA, Simone D. J. Interaçao humano-computador - Rio de Janeiro : Elsevier, 2010.

STROBEL, Karin. **As imagens do outro sobre a cultura surda-** Florianópolis: Ed. Da UFSC,2008.

SILVA, Renata Gabriela Galdino da. **A gastronomic guide for Caruaru: an essential service for tourism in the city** Caruaru : FAVIP, 2009.

UNGER, Russ; CHANDLER, Carolyn. **The user experience (UX) for designers of digital content, applications and web sites.** 1. ed. Rio de Janeiro: Editora alta books, 2009.

ANNEX 1

EVALUATION OF THE CARUARU TOURIST APP

GRADUATE: Iara Càssia de Melo Florêncio

ACTIVITIES IN THE TEST - **Usability Guia de Caruaru**

1-Name ____

2- Age __________

3- Find information about **the Caroà factory museum**.

( ) Performed

( ) Not done

4- Find the address of the **Severino Montenegro Environmental Park.**

( ) Performed

( ) Not done

5- Is the brief history of the city easy to understand?

( ) Performed

( ) Not done

6- Find the opening hours of **Baraûnas Park.**

( ) Performed

( ) Not done

Printed by Books on Demand GmbH, Norderstedt / Germany